HANWELL & SOUTHALL

THROUGH TIME

Paul Howard Lang

AMBERLEY

This book is dedicated to Colin Harris and Louise Eldridge

First published 2017

Amberley Publishing
The Hill, Stroud, Gloucestershire, GL5 4EP
www.amberley-books.com

Copyright © Paul Howard Lang, 2017

The right of Paul Howard Lang to be identified as the
Author of this work has been asserted in accordance with
the Copyrights, Designs and Patents Act 1988.

ISBN 978 1 4456 5494 2 (print)
ISBN 978 1 4456 5495 9 (ebook)

British Library Cataloguing in Publication Data.
A catalogue record for this book is available from the
British Library.

Origination by Amberley Publishing.
Printed in Great Britain.

Acknowledgements

David Blackwell
Phillip Edney
Louise Eldridge
Colin Harris
Charles Jobson
Tasmin Lang
Vincent Neale
Jonathan Oates

SOUTHALL STATION.

Introduction

The majority of the images in this book can be dated to the Edwardian period (1901–14), and in many ways it was this era that was the most significant in the development of Hanwell and Southall. Their populations doubled between 1901 and 1911. Hanwell's population grew from 10,438 in 1901 to 19,129 in 1911 and Southall's went from 10,438 to 26,323 – huge increases in such a short time. It was in the same period that electric trams made their appearance and revolutionised transport. Industry expanded in Southall while, to a lesser extent, light industry grew in Hanwell. Hanwell amalgamated with Ealing in 1926 and with Southall in 1965, but they still have their own identities today, as they did a hundred years ago.

Many houses were built at this time and are laid out in the grid work of urban development that is familiar to us today. Before the Edwardian era, both Southall and Hanwell had largely been agricultural areas. The image of Southall High Street showing a wagon laden down with hay exemplifies this transitional period.

The ninety old images in this book have been ordered into a walking tour of Hanwell and Southall. This starts at Brent Bridge as the River Brent is the boundary between the two parishes. With a slight detour to view the Hanwell locks, the route travels eastward showing the significant buildings along the Hanwell Broadway. The most northerly point shows the former Central London District School's building, now Hanwell Community Centre. The Hanwell tour ends at its most southerly border with Boston Manor, with an incredibly rural view of the Boston Road, which is hard to equate to the modern scene and is perhaps the most striking contrast in the book.

There have been more pictures of Southall, probably because it is the larger parish with an area of 2,608 acres compared to Hanwell's 992. The images of Southall start just past the River Brent, showing the viaduct. The tour continues westwards, taking a diversion down Dormers Wells Lane, the most westerly point, and goes right up to Hayes Bridge. Proceeding along the Grand Union Canal, it finally finishes at Norwood Green. The very last image shows 'Top Locks' in Southall, not far from Brent Bridge (the starting point), so a grand circular tour is completed.

Many of the postcard photographs were published locally. The Vaux's Stores shown in The Broadway, Hanwell, produced many images; the picture of the Hanwell fire brigade taken in 1896, although not published until the Edwardian period, is a good example. Southall's most prolific photographer and producer of cards was

John King, whose premises at No. 12 High Street can be seen in the image showing the Three Horse Shoes (his establishment is to the left of the public house).

While the majority of the period images are postcards, some photographs have also been used. Notably, these include the view of Hanwell looking west; the Boston Road shown at the end of the Hanwell section; and, in the Southall part, the fire at Endacott's, perhaps the most outstanding image in the book.

Some of the views featured in this book may be familiar to readers; however, I am sure that others will not be, for example the image of the Revd John Arthur Broadbelt by the King's Hall surrounded by the King's Hall Sisterhood.

For further reading I would suggest Dr Jonathan Oates' book *Southall and Hanwell: History and Guide* (2003), an excellent up-to-date account. Also Peter Hounsell's *Ealing and Hanwell Past* (1991) is a good guide to nineteenth-century Hanwell. As to more antiquarian accounts, Sir Montagu Sharpe's *Some Account of Bygone Hanwell* (1924) is of interest. Samuel Short's *Southall and Its Environs* (1910) is the first book dealing with the town's history. R. J. Mead's *Growing-up with Southall from 1904* is also an interesting memoir of this area.

MAYPOLE MARGARINE WORKS.
SOUTHALL, MIDDLESEX.

Maypole Margarine Works

An aerial view of the margarine works, clearly showing its good transport links and the unspoilt rural surrounds. The factory opened in 1895 and closed in 1929. It was owned by Otto Monsted Ltd, a firm of Danish origin. Note, however, the British flag flying above the works.

Bird's-Eye View from Water Tower, Southall.

A Bird's-Eye View from Water Tower, Southall

A good view of the railway station and Maypole margarine works. The houses on the left are in The Crescent and were demolished in 2016. The railway goods yard can also be seen on the left, where a number of coal merchants operated and livestock would arrive by rail for the weekly livestock market.

HANWELL

Brent Bridge — Hanwell

Vaux series

Brent Bridge, Hanwell

The previous Brent Bridge of four brick-built arches was 31 feet 9 inches wide between the parapets. The bridge was maintained by the bishop of London, who was lord of the manor of Hayes until around the 1830s. Norwood/Southall were part of Hayes parish until 1859. It was rebuilt and widened by the Trustees of the Uxbridge Turnpike in 1762 and was repaired by the county in 1815. Access to the Hanwell bank of the River Brent is now barred, so this had to be photographed from the Southall side. In the intervening years the vegetation has proliferated, so a closer view of the current bridge had to be taken.

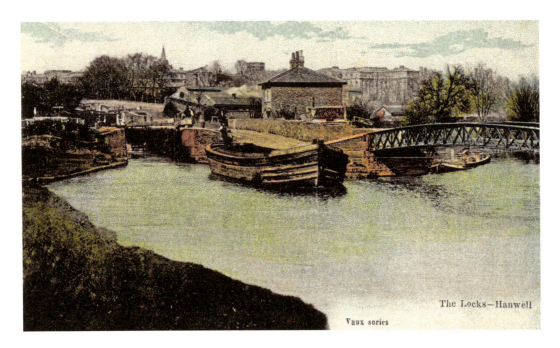

The Locks—Hanwell

Vaux series

The Locks, Hanwell

The confluence of the River Brent with the Grand Union Canal (formerly the Grand Junction Canal until 1929) just below Lock 97. This lock is on the left-hand side of the 1905 picture; beyond this the Hanwell flight of locks climbs beside the perimeter walls of the former asylum, the buildings of which can be seen in the background. The Brent River was canalised to create a navigable waterway. Although called the Hanwell Locks, actually they are on the Southall side of the border. The lock-keeper's cottage can also be seen in the centre of the image. In the modern photograph, Ealing Hospital now stands out as the dominant building.

Coffee House, Uxbridge Road, Hanwell

Kate Neighbour owned this coffee shop at No. 200 Uxbridge Road on the corner of Lower Boston Road – it is probably her standing in the doorway in this image. In 1901 Kate lived close by in Station Road with her husband William, their son and daughter aged five and seven and an eighteen-year-old servant called Sydney Pearce. This image is from around 1910 when Kate was forty-three years old. Her husband William may be the person tinkering with the motorcycle, which has been identified as a Peugeot. By 1911 the Neighbour family was living in Hayes. A dental laboratory now occupies this building. Note the film poster on the right of the shop advertising 'Sexton Blake in Ealing'. Sexton Blake was a fictional British detective.

Station Road, Hanwell

Station Parade was built in 1901 and from the start the refreshment rooms, owned by Mr Edward George Talbot, were on the corner nearest to Laurel Gardens. This shop is on the extreme left of the picture; next came a hairdressers owned by Mr Alfred Jones, then a tobacconist managed by John Charles Sledge. A dairyman, stationer and bootmaker followed, with general stores on the corner of Myrtle Gardens. The current photograph shows that the shops are all rather nondescript in comparison with the Edwardian view. Only the first projecting roof finial still remains.

Hanwell Broadway Looking West

This view of Hanwell Broadway shows the Uxbridge Road looking westwards, with the London County Asylum faintly visible in the background. The London & South Western Bank is on the extreme right; Mr Bramwell was the manager in 1905. The chemist between the bank and the pub had been managed by Mr Rippon. The Duke of York public house was a recognised staging point and omnibus terminus later on. The first building on the left-hand side by the tram was a butchers owned by John Goddard. However, the focal point is the round traffic island with the four distinctive lamps in the foreground.

The Broadway, Hanwell

The Broadway, Hanwell
Positioned in a strategic location was Vaux's Stores in Hanwell, seen here in 1908. The store was owned by John Campbell. Vaux's was a gentleman's outfitters and cycle maker from 1888 until 1916. Vaux published a variety of images of local scenes and sold them as postcards, many featuring in this book. The former stores have, in more recent times, been a computer shop and are currently a food store. A plaque to Jim Marshall, who pioneered electric amplification, can be seen on the wall of this building.

Hanwell Broadway

Taken from the corner of Boston Road, this view of Hanwell Broadway is from the late 1960s. The Duke of York public house is on the extreme left-hand side. The two shops between the pub and Barclays bank are Mr V. G. Peters, a watchmaker, and Rex Renovations Ltd. Ye Olde Hanwell Stores is on the right-hand side, the proprietor being Henry Carter. It was classed as a wine store but also sold general goods. In the current view we can see that the former bank is now a pizza shop and the old store is now the Clocktower Café.

Published by J. C. Vaux,   **Hanwell Broadway, 1896.**   *Hanwell.*

Hanwell Broadway, 1896

Hanwell got its first steam fire engine in 1879, before either Southall or Ealing owned one. Governance came under the Board of Lighting Inspectors at that time. The fire engine itself was housed in a shed at the rear of the Victoria Hotel in Boston Road, and the horses hired from a cab yard behind the Duke of York Hotel. In 1892 the fire station in Cherington Road was erected and the engine and equipment were housed there. The picture shows the horse-drawn fire engine in Hanwell Broadway with Cherington Road behind.

Uxbridge Road, Hanwell

The shops on the north side of Hanwell Broadway are seen here in the 1960s. On the extreme right is Robert's, a wool shop, and next to that is E. E. Ball, a newsagents. The shop that stands out with the unusual sign above the darker canopy is Barnkels, a motor spares shop. Next is Avon Electrics, followed by The Regent, a tobacco and confectionery shop. Note the lack of restrictions regarding parking in this period. A minicab firm, Chick'n'Spice, an accountants and Ealing Fabrics currently occupy the former shops.

ST. JOSEPH'S CONVALESCENT HOME, HANWELL.

St Joseph's Convalescent Home, Hanwell

St Joseph's Convalescent Home for women and children postdates the nearby Roman Catholic Church of St Joseph's in Hanwell. The first director was a Miss Barton in 1897, then a Miss Falls in 1898. The image shown here was taken in 1914 while Miss Mary Frances Baker was the matron (1899–1919). In 1901 there were five convalescents, two servants and two boarders (all female). From 1923 onwards it was St Mary's Convent, with the superbly named Sister Annunciata as superior in the 1920s and 1930s. The former building was demolished in the 1960s and a new convent erected as a replacement.

Hanwell Public Library

Sir Clifton Robinson was the managing director of the London United Tramway Company. He opened Hanwell public library in what was then Church Road West (now Cherington Road) on the 27 September 1905. Sir Clifton and Lady Robinson were received at the entrance of the library by the chairman and members of the District Council and the Library Committee; the opening took place in the lecture room. The first librarian appointed was Mr Frank Pocock. The books were on closed access and so had to be individually requested. Many changes to the library have taken place over the intervening years, but fortunately the building, which is an Andrew Carnegie bequest, has remained.

Opening of the Carnegie Public Library, Hanwell, by
SIR CLIFTON ROBINSON,
On Wednesday,   27th September, 1905.

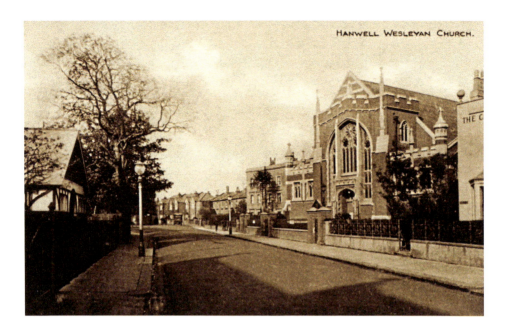

Wesleyan Church, Hanwell

The Commercial & Maritime Engine Co. Ltd building is on the extreme right, beside the church. They were in business from 1913–25, which roughly dates the picture. The engineering works had taken over 'Oak Villa', a former private residence. The Wesleyan church at Hanwell was in the Lower Boston Road from 1884, but was relocated to Church Road in 1904, opening on the 9 November that year. The architects were Gordon and Gunton. The building is of red brick with gothic pinnacles. The modern photograph shows that a strikingly modern building, the Hanwell Health Centre, has replaced the former building that stood next to the Methodist church.

Church Road, Hanwell

This unusual view of Church Road is dated 1915, most views of this road being taken in the opposite direction. Notice the small direction sign to the church attached to the sewage ventilation shaft post. The Methodist church is on the left with two boys posing for the camera. St Mellitus Church is on the right, with its distinctive bell cote. The church was built in 1910, the architect being Sir Arthur Blomfield & Sons. The building is in a Gothic Revival style. The entrance to Cherington Road is marked by the small island and post on the extreme right-hand side.

Conolly Dell

This unusually wild and rather haunting image of Conolly Dell is from 1915. The Dell's 1.5 acres were opened to the public in 1912. The memorial to John Conolly, M.D., in the grounds of the Dell explains that the gardens of 'The Lawn', Conolly's former house, have now become this beautifully landscaped public park. Dr Conolly was the third superintendent of the county asylum situated on the Southall side of the Brent Bridge nearby. The modern photograph shows the improvements that have been made to the layout of the grounds and the small lakes.

PUBLISHED BY GOLDEN MANOR, HANWELL. *Wakefields* EALING, W

Golden Manor, Hanwell

Although the names Golden Manor and Manor Court Road would seem to imply that Hanwell had a manor house, this was not the case. In fact, the manor courts were held in Greenford until the eighteenth century. The Golden Manor estate dates to the 1890s and contained a number of large houses for middle-class residents, who undoubtedly commuted by train to London. The modern photograph shows that although the road has ostensibly changed in appearance, with some blocks of flats replacing detached houses, it is still a pleasant tree-lined thoroughfare.

Recreation Grounds, Hanwell

Hanwell has a lower proportion of open space than Southall, but each of its parks has its own individual character. Churchfields is the open space to the south of Hanwell's parish church and was Hanwell's first public park, which opened in 1898. It is an undulating area that slopes up to fine vistas from its highest point. Brent Lodge Park is known locally as the 'Bunny Park' because of its animal centre. The other parks in Hanwell are Elthorne Park, Conolly Dell and King George's Fields; all are charming but relatively small areas. The modern photograph shows how the trees have grown up over the intervening years.

Hanwell, Parish Church

Hanwell Parish Church

There are many images of St Mary's, Hanwell's parish church, but this colour one from 1905 shows the surrounding trees, epitomising the rural aspect of the parish. The church was designed by Sir Gilbert Scott and W. B. Moffatt and was built in 1841. It was one of Gilbert Scott's first commissions and replaced a Georgian building. Many sources claim that the church was founded in AD 958; although this is a possibility, it is more likely that the original church dates to the twelfth century. A little-known fact is that in the medieval period the church ran an alehouse to help the parish funds. Notable frescoes by William Yeames R.A. are to be found in the chancel, as the artist lived nearby in Campbell Road. A memorial to Jonas Hanway, who popularised the umbrella, can also be found in the church. The current photograph shows how the trees have grown to partially obscure the view.

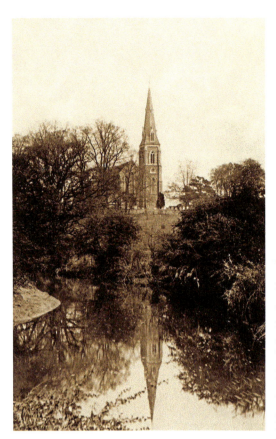

The Brent River, Hanwell

After appropriately running through the borough of Brent, the Brent River enters the borough of Ealing at West Twyford, flowing westwards through Perivale and Greenford, before turning south through Greenford, Hanwell and Southall. Importantly, the river forms the boundary between Southall and Hanwell, becoming the Grand Union Canal south of Ealing Hospital and finally flowing down into Brentford to merge with the Thames. The river has often been polluted in the past and is too small for boats. As the river is fairly shallow along the majority of its length, it has not been exploited to its full potential and remains one of the less well-known rivers of London. The current photograph shows that this picturesque river still remains a haven for wildlife.

Boles Bridge, Hanwell

It is uncertain how the name 'Boles' came about and there were alternative names for this bridge – Bowles and Bulls among others. This image clearly shows a wooden structure so must predate 1954 when the metal one was substituted. The wooden bridge, which crosses the Brent River, needed replacing in 1905, and after many months Southall Council finally agreed to go halves with Hanwell in funding this project, which was settled in October 1905. The current photograph shows that the path leading to the bridge has changed course and vegetation now covers the previously open land leading to it.

Golf Course Entrance, Hanwell

It is immediately apparent how little this scene has changed over the years. The triangular-shaped green still remains and gives a quaint aspect to the area. To the right is Cuckoo Lane and to the left Church Road. The oldest building in Hanwell 'Crossways' of the late eighteenth century can be seen on the right of the pictures. The gates to the Brent Valley Golf Course are behind the green in the centre of the picture. The golf club dates back to 1936. The 'Little Lodge' building to the right of the entrance to the club has pointed, Gothic-style windows. In many ways the golf course has helped preserve the semi-rural seclusion of this part of Hanwell.

Grove Avenue, Hanwell

When Hanwell Park estate was broken up into two parts, Brent Park and Hanwell Grove, the latter became the Grove Estate. The building of what would later become Grove Avenue started in March 1900, with the first plots of houses on the east side. It was not until February 1902 that two houses were actually named as being in Grove Avenue. In November 1902 the houses along the east side of the avenue had been completed. Grove Avenue was complete by 1914, apart from the top end on the east side. The final houses were completed in 1934. The picture shown here is from 1915.

PARK HOTEL, HANWELL

Park Hotel, Greenford Avenue

The Park Hotel, seen here in 1904, was designed by the architect Mr George Henry Pargeter (1864–1934), composed of red brick with Bath-stone enrichments, the upper portion being relieved with minarets. The Park Hall had a separate entrance and could accommodate an audience of 500. It was multifunctional, hosting concerts, plays and films were also shown here later on. The building was erected in ten months by Messrs Speechley & Smith, contractors of Richmond; the entire furnishings and fittings were supplied by John Sanders of Ealing Broadway. The photograph below shows the residential buildings that have replaced the former hotel.

Milton Road, Hanwell

Tennyson, Milton, Shakespeare and Cowper roads, known collectively as 'Poets' Corner', lay on the east side of Greenford Avenue. There is another 'Poets' Corner' in Acton. Mr Campbell Johnstone bought land that was formerly Hanwell Park Estate and sold it for housing in July 1903. It was specified that houses, detached and semi-detached, must have a value of more than £300 to attract the middle classes. Shakespeare Road was completed by 1910 but Milton Road was not; like Grove Avenue the houses along Milton Road were built in sections. Note the young saplings planted on the right-hand side of the picture and the complete absence of vehicles and people.

Beechmount Avenue, Greenford Avenue, Hanwell.

Beechmount Avenue, Hanwell

Beechmount Avenue and the surrounding roads off the Greenford Avenue were owned and constructed on railway land by the Great Western Land Co. Ltd. They had owned the land since 1912, and the whole area was promoted as 'Elthorne Heights'. Originally, a park was planned but never created. The Beechmount Avenue houses were started in October 1927. This building programme culminated in 1938 when Gifford Gardens was finally completed. The picture of Beechmount seen here is postmarked 11 January 1940 but is probably from an earlier period. Like many of these street scenes it is notable for a complete lack of cars and people.

"FARM AVENUE" CENTRAL LONDON DISTRICT SCHOOLS HANWELL W.7 137

Farm Avenue, 'Central London District Schools', Hanwell

Farm Avenue was the track leading from Ruislip Road East (then known as Greenford Road) to the Central London District Schools. The view has been taken looking north, away from the school and towards Cuckoo Farm; this was sited at the junction between Ruislip Road East and Greenford Avenue. The school reservoir can be seen on the right-hand side along this beautiful horse chestnut-lined avenue. This view reminds us how rural Hanwell was in the Edwardian period. The modern view of the avenue, now renamed Cuckoo Avenue, shows that the reservoir and trees have gone, but it still retains some of its former charm.

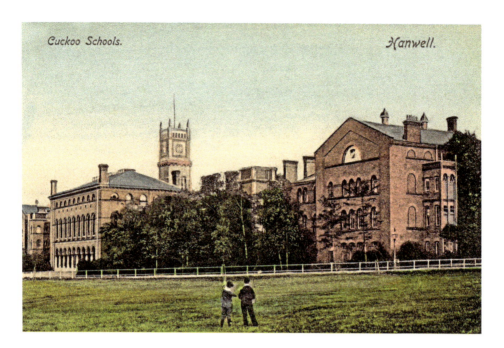

Cuckoo Schools.   Hanwell.

Cuckoo Schools, Hanwell

The Central London District Schools were located at Hanwell in 1856 and lasted until 1933. They were renamed the Hanwell Residential School from 1930 and known locally as the 'Cuckoo Schools', although the name cuckoo can be traced back to maps prior to 1850. A famous pupil from this school is Charlie Chaplin, who was here from June 1896 until January 1898. In his autobiography he describes the harsh discipline at the school, although this was customary at the time. The modern photograph shows that the east and west wings have now been demolished. The central administrative block of Italianate design still remains, as does the tower. It is now used as the Hanwell Community Centre.

St. George's Cemetery, Hanwell

St George's Cemetery, Hanwell

In the Victorian period, overcrowding in central London churchyards made it necessary to find locations for cemeteries outside of the metropolis. Hanwell has two examples of this type of cemetery: St George's and, on the other side of the Uxbridge Road, the Kensington and Chelsea Cemetery. The St George's or Westminster Cemetery was opened in 1854 and the architect was Robert Jerrard. The gatekeeper's lodge is on the left-hand side. Of note is a memorial inside the cemetery to Al Bowlly, the famous singer of the 1930s and 1940s, one of Britain's first popstars.

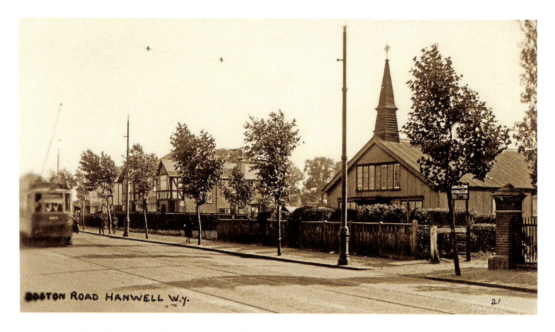

BOSTON ROAD HANWELL W.7.

21

Boston Road, St Thomas's Church, Hanwell

On the right-hand side is the temporary Church of St Thomas the Apostle, having been built on land given by the Earl of Jersey in 1909. The new church was completed in 1934, designed by the architect Sir Edward Maufe (1882–1974). If the architectural design of the new church looks familiar, it is because this church was built as a prototype for the cathedral at Guildford. The other interesting feature is the sculpture of Calvary made by Eric Gill on the east wall. Note the sign for Hanwell Town Football Club on the extreme right next to the park.

Boston Road, Hanwell

The most defined contrast in the book is captured in these two images of Boston Road. The rural scene could hardly be more different than the image of the houses and shops that had sprung up by 1935. This shows how the nearby railway station of Boston Manor fostered urban development in this area. Boston Road was originally called Boston Lane and, on a map from 1865, Boston Farm is indicated near this spot. The scene is right at the southern boundary and is the only part of the road that curves in this manner. The early photograph must have been taken before 1906 as there are no tramlines. Where the shops now stand has previously been allotments.

SOUTHALL

Wharncliffe Viaduct

The viaduct was named after Lord Wharncliffe, the chairman of the Parliamentary Committee on the Great Western Bill. The viaduct is 300 yards long and crosses the River Brent; it was Isambard Kingdom Brunel's first large-scale railway design. The Great Western Railway gained parliamentary approval in 1835, opening to Maidenhead in 1838 and to Bath in 1840. A special train took Queen Victoria and Prince Albert across the viaduct, with Brunel on the footplate a few years after the line was completed. The viaduct was doubled in width in 1877. The playground has now gone and has been relocated to the top of the hill.

The Asylum, Hanwell

hope you got home safe after the cat-chase
A. Parker

The Asylum

The Middlesex County Asylum, colloquially known as Hanwell Asylum, was technically in the precinct of Norwood (Southall). This unusual asymmetrical view of the asylum shows the gatehouse on the left-hand side, and the main octagonal tower beyond the trees. The asylum chapel can be seen on the right and even one of the paths on the female side of the asylum. The institution was opened in 1831, designed by the architect William Anderson and built by William Cubitt. The picture also shows how peaceful the Uxbridge Road was in the Edwardian period compared to the busy road it has now become. Notice the bare plot of land in the foreground, now filled with housing.

London County Asylum (in Southall-Norwood Parish), Nearest Railway Station, G.W.R. Hanwell. Postal Address—Hanwell, W.

Asylum Gatehouse

The gate porter can be seen standing in front of the asylum gatehouse in around 1904. He resided at the entrance lodge situated just to the right of the gateway. Beyond his house were the magistrates' stables. On the left-hand side of the gatehouse was the counting house and office and beyond that the engineers house. In 1901 there were two gate porters, Arnold William Cooley and George Alfred Colton. The gate porter was an important member of staff because he controlled access into the asylum and prevented patients escaping. He weighed all incoming carts and examined all parcels for contraband items. In the modern photograph, we can see that the central lamp over the gateway is now missing. The gatehouse was damaged during the Second World War but has since been repaired.

Hanwell Asylum. (II).

Published by I. C. Vaux, Hanwell

Hanwell Asylum

Two asylum officials can be seen outside the chapel on the main drive, with autumnal trees flanking either side of the drive. The chapel is perfectly framed in the middle. This was built by Henry Martin, the asylum's resident engineer in 1870, reputedly taking only eleven months to construct. The dedication took place on the 11 November 1870 by Bishop Claughton. It must be remembered how important the chapel and chaplain would have been in regard to the life of the asylum in the nineteenth century. The modern photograph shows the current building work in progress, the land having been sold to developers.

The Three Bridges, Southall

One of the last great engineering works undertaken by Isambard Kingdom Brunel is shown here. Brunel died soon after the project was completed in 1859. Coincidentally, one of Brunel's first major structures, the construction of the Wharncliffe viaduct, is not far from the Three Bridges, lying to the north of the asylum. The asylum grounds are at the top of this colourful picture, showing trees and a shelter. Although called the Three Bridges, there are actually only two. The canal crosses over the railway in an iron trough and the road crosses above the canal. There cannot be many places where road, railway and canal all intersect in this way. Access to the railway embankment where the photographer took this shot is now denied, so the current photograph had to be taken from the top of the road bridge looking down onto the canal and railway.

Golf Club, Southall.

The Golf Club, Southall

The West Middlesex Gold Club was founded in 1890. The course lies on both sides of the Greenford Road and is bounded in part by the River Brent. Originally the land, part of the vast Osterley Park Estate, was owned by the Earl of Jersey. This picture shows the original location of the golf club building, which was further south than the present-day clubhouse. The course is almost 200 acres and is nearly 5 miles round. The course was bought in 1938 by Middlesex County Council and Southall Borough Council and leased back to the club. The clubhouse suffered several fires but fortunately kept going. The current photograph shows where the original clubhouse used to stand.

DORMERS WELLS LANE   SOUTHALL   MDX.   GLOVER PHOTO

Dormers Wells Lane, Southall

The name 'Dormers Wells' can be traced back to 1384 when it appears in a court roll as 'Dormoteswell'. Much later on, the name was corrupted to Dorman's Wells and finally to Dormers Wells. Settlement goes back to Saxon times as pottery relating to this period was found near to Dormers Wells Farm, the outbuildings of which can be seen on the left of this picture. The view of the lane is from the north looking south, showing the pronounced curve in the road. Even by 1914, there were only the farm buildings and twelve houses on the west side of the lane. In 1914 it was actually called Dormers Wells Road but had changed to Lane by the 1930s.

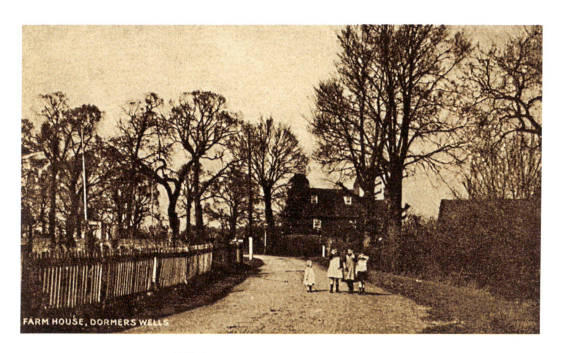

FARM HOUSE, DORMERS WELLS

Farm House, Dormers Wells Lane

The drive leading to Dormers Wells Farm can be seen in this Edwardian view. The farm consisted of the farm buildings themselves, Dormers Wells House and Dormers Wells Cottage. In 1914 the house was owned by Harry Rountree, the cottage was owned by Robert Watts and the farmer, Mr William Ewer, called himself a cattle dealer. In 1935 Mr Rountree was still living in the house, Jasper Royland Kinsey was the owner of the cottage and the dairy farm was owned by Snell & Sons. The current photograph shows that Farm Close, with residential houses, has now replaced the former buildings.

Holy Trinity Church, Southall

Holy Trinity Church stands on the corner of Park View Road and Uxbridge Road. The church was built in 1890 and designed by the architect J. W. T. Lee. The builder was J. Dorey, who also built St Mellitus Church in Hanwell. The exterior of the building has brick and stone facing and the interior has polychrome brick. It has an apsidal baptistery and has some war damage to the glass. The foundation stone was laid on the 5 June 1890 and it was consecrated on 31 January 1891. This building replaced a previous iron church building that dated to 1868. The current photograph shows that the vicarage building, although no longer used for this purpose, has remained unaltered and is still recognisable from the older scene.

The Sanatorium,
Mount Pleasant, Southall.

The Sanatorium, Mount Pleasant

The Sanatorium opened in 1904, having previously been a fever hospital. It was run by Dr Jabez Davenport Windle, a doctor in Southall for forty-one years and was also the Medical Officer for Health for Southall, a police surgeon and a doctor at the Hayes Jewish Industrial School. Miss Elizabeth West was the matron of the Sanatorium, which had sixty-eight beds when it opened. The Sanatorium survived into the 1980s and was demolished around 1991. Manor Court Care Home now stands in Britten Drive, as can be seen in the current photograph.

The Almshouses, Southall

The Almshouses, Southall

William Welch Deloitte (1818–98), who founded the famous accountancy firm, commissioned these six almshouses to be built in North Road, Southall, to mark Queen Victoria's Diamond Jubilee in 1897. Deloitte was a very philanthropic man, also giving money to Holy Trinity Church in Southall. He lived at Hill House, Mount Pleasant, which was said to command 'one of the prettiest views in Middlesex'. This view of the almshouses is from 1944; the only difference now is that the grassy patch of land opposite the almshouses has now been built on.

The Park, Southall

Southall Park House, the gardens of which would later form the basis of the park, was constructed in 1702 for Sarah Jennings. The eastern half of the park did not form part of the Southall Park House Estate. The house was later used as a private asylum by Sir William Ellis in 1838–39. After his death, his wife Mrs Mabel Ellis took over the running of this establishment from 1839–51. Dr Boyd became the superintendent in 1881 but the house burnt down 1883. The fire killed one of Dr Boyd's children, two patients, a domestic cook and the doctor himself. The burnt-out ruin of the house remained for several years after the event. The tragedy helped establish the Southall Fire Brigade. The gardens were purchased by the Urban District Council in 1909 and were converted into a public park.

THE LAKE, SOUTHALL PARK

The Lake, Southall Park

This unusual image of the lake is from the mid-1920s, the lake having been constructed in 1923. Unfortunately, in 1955 the lake was filled in on cost grounds and grassed over. In the 1940s there had been problems with the water seeping out, suggesting that the lake was in poor condition. The location can be determined by the clear view of Holy Trinity Church and Vicarage on the right-hand side beyond the trees. A long undulating depression in the grass indicates where the lake once was. The covering over of the bandstand can also be discerned at the western end of the lake. Notice the clever planting of the specimen trees at each end of the island, bookending the scene.

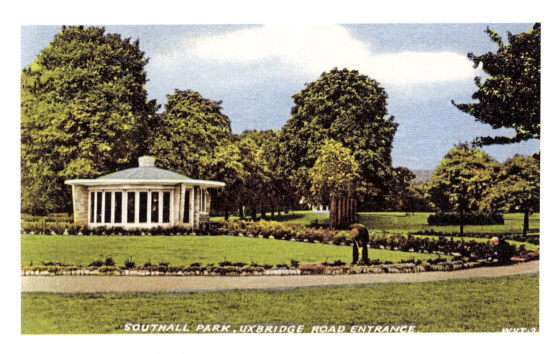

The Shelter, Southall Park

The Edwardian period was the heyday of the postcard; it is comparatively rare to find examples such as this from the 1960s. This image shows the circular shelter that stood roughly in the centre of the park, not far from the main entrance in the Uxbridge Road. The shelter was opened on the 8 June 1956 and was built on the former bandstand site. The estimated cost of construction was £1,300 and there were concerns regarding the cost of heating this structure at the time. The shelter was renovated in 1972, so had presumably been vandalised. It was finally pulled down after it suffered from further vandalism in May 1977. The current photograph shows where the former shelter once stood.

The County School, Southall

Erected in 1907, the Southall County Grammar School was a public secondary school for boys and girls situated in Villiers Road, by Boyd Avenue. The school magazine for 1911 shows that as well as obtaining high academic achievements the school also excelled in sporting activities. In 1914 the headmaster was Mr Samuel Pollitt BSc. He had seven assistant masters and five assistant mistresses. The art master was Mr Watson and the cookery teacher was Miss Bedell. In September 1963 there were 834 children on the roll, ranging in age from eleven to eighteen. Notice the two female pupils standing outside the building. It is now known as Villiers Road High School.

The White Hart, Southall

Opposite to the cattle market in the High Street stood the White Hart, pictured here in 1905. Because of the proximity to the cattle market, the pub had a special licence that allowed it to stay open at irregular hours. Like the Red Lion close by, it had been a posting house in the coaching era. Richardson, in his *Old Inns of England*, describes The White Hart as a fine house of early Georgian character. Regrettably, the original building was demolished in 1934. It was rebuilt but closed in 2009 and was demolished shortly after. In the current photograph the white hoardings are where The White Hart once stood.

The Red Lion, Southall

Fortunately the person sending the card has written September 1932 on the reverse side, so the image cannot post date this. The Red Lion stands next to Southall Park, which can be seen on the left. Note the workmen standing on the roof of the hotel and the boarded-up shop on the extreme right-hand side. At this time the proprietor was James Carr and the hotel had tea gardens, no doubt to show its refinement. The Red Lion acted as a posting house in the Victorian period, with many coaches stopping at this establishment. The coach to Thame in Oxfordshire stopped here, as did coaches to Hereford and Cheltenham. In the current photograph, we can see that a bright restaurant advertisement is now to the right of The Red Lion.

SOUTHALL MARKET IN 1805.

SOUTHALL MARKET, as here depicted, is of great interest from its institution, two centuries since, to the present day. In 1698, King William III. granted a charter to Francis Merrick, Esq. to hold a weekly market and two Fairs annually. In 1805, a lease was conveyed to Mr. William Welch, who laid out the sum of £1277 6s. 4d. in establishing a permanent enclosure as shown in the above picture. It became so frequented, that the old markets of Hayes and Hounslow were eventually considerably reduced in importance, and its popularity so great that it was the largest Fat Cattle Market in importance next to Smithfield. To Mr. J. Dale of the "George and Dragon" we are indebted for the privilege of reproducing this interesting old print, the original being in his possession.

PRESENT DAY.

Southall Market

A charter for a market in Southall was granted to Francis Merrick (1657–1702) by William III in 1698. The charter endorsed a weekly market dealing in grain, horses and cattle. Southall became very well known for the sale of horses. The older image, showing two different phases of development, is of interest as it gives a brief history of Southall Market. The modern photograph shows that a market is still thriving to this day, although now occupying a much-reduced site and no longer selling livestock.

The Town Hall, Southall

The Earl of Jersey donated the land for the town hall, which opened in 1897. Prior to this, Miss Staniford had offered a site in Southall Green, on which stood 'The Romans', but this was rejected by the Norwood/Southall Urban District Council. This view is from 1938 and shows how the glass canopy over the entrance spoils the architectural features of the building. Furthermore, the two toilets either side of the canopy are very prominent and could have been more discretely placed. Also note the old fire station next to the town hall. The former town hall is now used as a conference facility and the Southall Community Alliance is based in this building.

THE BROADWAY, SOUTHALL.

The Broadway, Southall I

This 1907 view of The Broadway shows Butler's, the gentlemen's outfitters, on the extreme left-hand side. The junction with South Road is where the three men, one with a bicycle, are talking. On the other side of the road, beyond the men with the handcart, is the sign for Auctioneer & Estate Offices of Francis Wakeling. Notice the armchairs arrayed outside the premises; they belonged to Symonds & Co, furniture dealers. A clothes shop now occupies the former establishment. A sign for teas can be seen just beyond the shop awnings.

H. J. BUTLER & Co's New Tailoring Premises,

THE BROADWAY, SOUTHALL.

(late LEGGETT'S FORGE.)

The New Corner.

The Old Corner.

The Broadway, Southall II

This trade card from H. J. Butler & Co. shows the striking contrast between the old rural site and the new retail one. In fact, one can hardly tell that Leggett's Forge once stood on this spot. In the older view, one can clearly see the sign for the Three Horse Shoes on the extreme right of the picture. During the First World War, not only did many of the Butler employees join up for active service, but Butler's also commissioned the Southall Roll of Honour, an invaluable list of the Southall men who had enlisted in 1914–15, regrettably never updated. The modern photograph shows that the view is still a busy area full of retail outlets.

The Broadway, Southall III

This good view of the shops on the south side of The Broadway is from 1911. The Broadway Stationers and Bookshop on the extreme right was owned by Charles Henry Prideaux. The shop next to that was owned by Frederick Joseph Hallam, a corn chandler, with a sign for Spratt's patent puppy biscuits in the window. Next to Hallam's was a grocers belonging to the Thomas Brothers. A photographic studio owned by Charles Gray could be found above the grocers. These former shops are now, from right to left, a shoe shop, Sunny Centre, an opticians and Meet Brothers shop.

High Street, Southall I

This Edwardian view of the high street shows the different types of transport that were popular at this time. The horse and cart carrying hay reminds us that agricultural pursuits still went on, while the Co-operative cart tells us about retail trade in the area. Notice also the tramlines in the road, which date this image after 1901. Several bicycles can also be seen, a popular means of transportation. The shop on the extreme right called Langler was a drapers, owned by two Southall-born ladies, Elizabeth and May Ann Langler. The modern view shows what a vast increase in traffic there is in comparison with the sedate Edwardian view.

High Street, Southall II

The shop with the large pocket watch-style sign on the right-hand side belonged to John Henry Davis. Next to that, on the corner of Avenue Road, was a butchers owned by the Jiggens Brothers, who also owned a shop on the north side of the road at No. 17. The imposing building with the turret at the top on the other side of Avenue Road was a Barclay's bank; the manager in 1914 was Mr Percival Mallinson. The delivery cart has probably come from the Red Lion Hotel further down the street. Delights, a shop selling waffles, crepes and milkshakes, now occupies the former bank premises.

High Street, Southall III

A 1905 view of the high street showing how busy this part of Southall was; notice the lack of traffic and how people felt safe enough to walk in the middle of the road at this time. The view shows Barton's the confectioners on the extreme right. Next to that was a greengrocer owned by Alfred Durbin, and Wells shop can just be made out, the second shop past the greengrocers. This was a stationer's shop managed by Mrs Emily Sophia Wells at No. 6 High Street. Currently a money transfer shop, a barbers, electrical hardware, jewellers, internet café, Betfred, another internet café and Nasina's chicken shop have now taken the place of the former shops.

The Three Horse Shoes, High Street, Southall

The old Three Horse Shoes was a beerhouse (beerhouses are off licences where alcholic drinks can be bought but not consumed on the premises) occupying part of Northcote House abutting on Southall Green Lane, now South Road. Thomas Gilbert Baxter was the landlord and he can be traced from 1914 to 1935; however, the first mention of the Three Horse Shoes as a public house did not come until 1924. The lack of earlier references is probably because it was only a beerhouse and therefore did not have a full licence. Looking down the High Street in 1914, the premises of John King, the printers, can be seen at No. 12, although he had moved by 1916 and another printer, Augustine Price, had taken over his establishment. John King owned offices at No. 76 King Street, Southall, as well as No. 213 Uxbridge Road, West Ealing, and No. 181A Uxbridge Road, Hanwell. He produced and sold many postcards of Southall, some of which are featured in this book.

Proprietor, J. DALE. **GEORGE AND DRAGON HOTEL.** Photo, ALFRED SMITH, Southall.

The George & Dragon, Southall

Mr Dale, the landlord of the George & Dragon, ran this establishment with his wife, two barmen and a female cook from 1905–15. He was born in Scotland in 1872 and was a freemason. When the George & Dragon opened in 1826, the licensee was Levi Puddifoot. The building lasted until the 1930s, when the old pub was replaced by a mock-Tudor three-storey building, which was itself demolished in 2005. Note the sundial positioned at the top of the building between the words Isleworth and Brewer. The sundial had the words 'Sic Transit Gloria' on its face. The pub was also renowned for its huge fireplace, which proved a great attraction in the winter months. The current photograph shows that Chana Chemist has now replaced the former building.

Paragon Palace, South Road

The Paragon Palace cinema is on the right-hand side of this view of South Road from 1920. The cinema was first known as the New Paragon Palace Cinematograph Theatre and its manager was Mr C. B. Roberts. The cinema had 300 seats and was built by Hansons, a local Southall firm. Regrettably, little is known about the building's architect. It opened in 1912, closed in 1928 and was demolished in 1929, when another cinema, called the Palace, took its place. The replacement cinema had an even more exotic architectural style, reflecting that of a Chinese pagoda. The current photograph shows that the Himalaya Palace shopping centre now occupies the site.

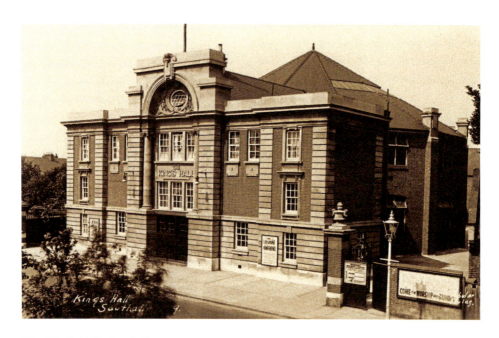

The King's Hall, Southall

This imposing building, looking architecturally as if it had been designed for some municipal purpose rather than as a church, can be found in South Road in Southall. The building dates to 1916 and was designed by Sir Alfred Gelder of Hull. The King's Hall served as a headquarters for the local Methodists and acted as a social, as well as a religious, meeting place. It later became a centre for Asian Christians, services in Hindi being conducted from 1974. Prior to this building there had been a former Wesleyan Methodist chapel in South Road dating to 1885. Sadly, the present building became defunct in 2013, owing mainly to high upkeep costs. The current photograph shows the building empty, abandoned and awaiting redevelopment.

Revd Broadbelt Outside King's Hall, Southall

The Revd Broadbelt can be seen with the King's Hall Sisterhood outside the King's Hall in South Street in June 1922. The poster on the gate pier refers to Dame Margaret Lloyd George, the wife of the then prime minister. Dame Margaret graciously agreed to patronise the King's Hall Sisterhood event. The ladies look on, expectantly awaiting her arrival. Due to heavy rain in the morning, the garden fete was moved from the Manor House grounds and held inside the King's Hall. Many stalls were manned by the Sisterhood, who hoped to raise money for their cause. The current photograph shows that the building is now in a somewhat neglected state.

St.MaryleboneSchools, Southall.   WH.A581.

St Marylebone School, Southall

Less well known than the Central London District School in Hanwell was the St Marylebone Parochial School, another London parish school that relocated to what was then the countryside. In the mid-Victorian period it was thought that poor children from central London schools would benefit from being moved to the fresh air of the countryside. The school opened in 1858 on the west side of South Road. In 1901 the superintendent was John Henry Edwards and his wife Susan Ellen was matron. The establishment held as many as 500 children at its peak. The image here is from around 1905. During the First World War the building was used as an Australian military hospital and afterwards was turned into a Roman Catholic girls' school. The current photograph shows that the former school building has been demolished (in the 1920s) and replaced with residential housing.

— *SOUTHALL HEAD POST OFFICE.*

Southall Head Post Office

Henry Charles Hanson was the head postmaster at this establishment from 1876 to 1907. He lived at 'The Lawns' in South Road and died on 20 March 1920, leaving £44,000 in his will. The post office rapidly expanded during his period of office. The head post office seen here had entrances in both South Road and Beaconsfield Road. This view is from around 1905. The Office of Works purchased the building in 1912. A new post office in the same location was opened in July 1938. Currently, the Punjab National Bank and other businesses now occupy the former post office building.

SOUTHALL STATION.

Southall Station

Fred Webster was the stationmaster at Southall from 1908 until 1930; before this he had been the stationmaster at Acton. He was born in 1864 in Thame in Oxfordshire and in 1911 lived at No. 17 Avenue Road in Southall. He was unmarried and lived with his widowed mother and two sisters. This image shows the station in 1911 with a clear view of the water tower in the centre of the image. In 1910 there were sixty-five trains running every day between Southall and Paddington.

OTTO MONSTED LIMITED. VIEW OF WORKS, SOUTHALL.

Otto Monsted Ltd, View of the Works, Southall

Southall was chosen as the location of the Maypole Margarine Works (the largest margarine factory in the whole of Europe at one time) because of its excellent transport links, having both canal and railway connections close by. Otto Monsted, the owner of the margarine factory, was Danish, as were all of his senior staff (Hanson's, the Southall building firm, was also Danish). The factory opened in 1895 and closed in 1929. The current photograph shows that although some of the factory buildings such as the offices and chimney have gone, a substantial range of buildings still remains. The end building on the left is possibly the most iconic, having been used as the former Sunrise Radio Station.

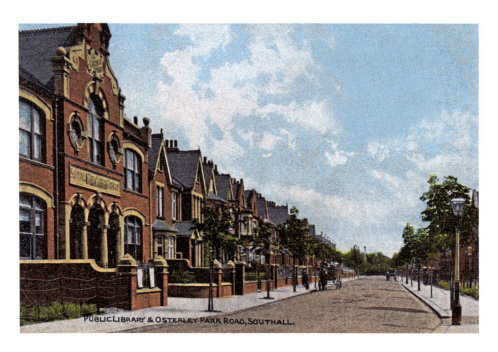

PUBLIC LIBRARY & OSTERLEY PARK ROAD, SOUTHALL.

Public Library and Osterley Park Road

Southall public library was officially opened on the 26 July 1905 by Mrs Bigwood, wife of Mr James Bigwood, MP. Lady Jersey performed the ceremony of laying the foundation stone in 1904. The philanthropist Andrew Carnegie bore the entire cost of the building, as he had also done for Hanwell public library. This image is from 1907 and, apart from the library, it shows the relatively middle-class residencies of the tree-lined Osterley Park Road. The current photograph shows the boarded-up library building, which closed in 2014; the library moved to the recently renovated Dominion Centre.

Manor House and Memorial, Southall

The war memorial was unveiled in 1922 and stands proudly near the Manor House. Hanwell has no similar war memorial but there is a small memorial in Churchfields Park commemorating the scouts who died in the First World War. Recently restored, the Manor House is the oldest buildings in Southall, established in the sixteenth century, originally belonging to the Awsiter family. An inventor of a unique type of sewing machine, William Thomas, also lived in this house. Today, the Manor House is Grade II listed, and a project is underway to convert parts of the interior into a catering establishment.

Manor Parade, Southall.

Manor Parade, Southall

Across the road from the Manor House and the war memorial stands Manor Parade. The group of shops pictured here in 1930 on the west side of the road were built on land from the former large house called 'The Romans'. That house was demolished in around 1923. The parade of shops consisted of a café owned by Eugenio Curo; fishmongers, Howard & Turner; greengrocers Jas Bedworth; United Dairies (London) Ltd; a shop selling gowns owned by Madam Adaire; and finally a boot repair and fish shop managed by H. B. Herman. The current photograph shows that these shops have now entirely changed.

KING ST. SOUTHALL.

King Street Showing Featherstone Hall

In this view from 1912, Featherstone Hall can be seen beyond the curving wall pierced with windows in the distance. Featherstone Hall was known by the locals as Welsh's Folly, as it was built by Alfred Welsh. This eccentric building cost £20,000 and took seven years to construct. It was used as a private lunatic asylum from 1891 when Hezekibah Dixon was the first proprietor. He had five servants, eight attendants and ten female patients. In 1911, William Henry Bailey, MD, DPH, was in charge. From 1925–32 Alfred Newman Leathem, MRCS, LRCP, managed the asylum. It was then demolished and the Dominion Cinema was opened in 1935.

St. John's Church and King Street, Southall

St John's Church and King Street, Southall

The Vitriol Works owner, Henry Dodds, was the prime mover in getting this church established. The church was originally a chapel of ease to Norwood Church and was consecrated by the Archbishop of Canterbury in 1841. The church underwent major repairs in 1891. By the end of the Edwardian period it was realised that, with the growing population at this time, the church would have to be replaced by a larger one, so a new church was constructed nearby in Church Avenue. As can be seen in the photograph, St John's awaits a new centre, which will incorporate the old building. The first stage involves resiting the gravestones and paving the areas in front of the church.

Endacott's During the Fire

The drapers store Endacott's in King Street (on the corner of Western Road) was severely damaged by fire on the 27 November 1914. The fire started in a back room, but its cause was never ascertained. The conflagration was attended by the Southall Fire Brigade, and the Ealing & Hanwell and Heston & Isleworth Brigades also came to the rescue. Mrs Endacott was trapped in an upstairs bedroom, but she was rescued by some telephone wiremen who happened to be working in Western Road. The store was entirely gutted but later restored. Endacott's stopped trading in 1924. The current photograph show that a Pound Plus store, Ram's Photographer and The London Jewellers now take the place of the former premises.

Platt's Stores, Southall

Platt's Stores started business in 1914 and continued until 1955. They were situated at Nos 44–48 King Street, Southall. The sign above the central section of their stores announces that they also had further shops at Hounslow, Kingston, Hammersmith, Mortlake and Brentford – so they covered quite a wide area. An early advertisement for Platt's describes their business as, 'Purveyors of Best English Meat Killed on Premises. Groceries, Provisions, Drugs & Patent Medicines, Ironmongery & Turnery.' In 1955, apart from the King Street stores, they owned shops at Crossland Parade, Norwood Green; Station Road, Hayes; and the High Street, Harlington. The current photograph shows that Tesco Express and a hair and beauty spa are now on the former site of Platt's.

Featherstone Road, Infant's & Boys School Southall.

Featherstone Road School, Southall

The Featherstone Road School is pictured here in 1908. Initially an infants' school founded in 1890, it was expanded in 1901 to include juniors and accommodated 500 boys. Mr West was the headmaster of the boys and Miss Nightingale the head of the infants. In 1963 there were 250 infants aged from five to seven and 333 mixed juniors aged from seven to eleven. By 1993 it had become a community primary school catering for three to eleven year olds. Perhaps the most famous pupil to attend this school was Cleo Laine, the jazz singer. The school was also attended by the mother of the Duchess of Cambridge, our future queen. The current photograph shows that the building has recently been converted to private residences.

Western Road, Southall

The Primitive Methodists had a chapel built on the corner of Western Road and Sussex Road in 1876–77. The building is in the centre of the picture. The chapel was registered in 1878 and was described as a two-storey building of yellow brick with a cement-rendered front. The minister in 1914 was Revd Charles Spooner. He held morning and evening services on Sundays and evening services on Thursdays. In 1985 the Western Road building became a Church of God Pentecostal chapel. The current view shows the changes that the shops have undergone.

Western Road School

The Western Road girls' school opened on the 28 August 1911 with 238 children. 130 children came from Featherstone Road, forty from Harlington Road and forty-eight from Clifton Road infant's schools respectively. Twenty were newly admitted children. The school has an unusual shape and the building was not completed on time, but four classrooms were made available. The head teacher of the infants was Miss Mary Jones, who was paid a salary of £140 per annum. School rambles and gardening, among more traditional subjects, featured in the curriculum. Miss Jones remained at the school until the end of September 1941. Note the war memorial in the modern picture on the left-hand side.

Canal Side from Hayes Bridge, Southall

Right at the western boundary with Hayes along the Uxbridge Road stands Hayes Bridge. A row of houses called 'Bankside' can be seen on the left-hand side. Bankside appears on a 1896 map standing on its own, before the roads running south from the Uxbridge Road, such as Beresford, Ranelagh and Woodlands Roads, had been laid out. Bankside was also known as Hambrough Cottages, which were occupied by labourers working in the brickfields and margarine factory. The gasworks can be seen in the distance, a site used in many 1970s TV shows such as *The Sweeney* and *The Professionals*. Just out of shot on the left stands the Hambrough Tavern that was burnt down in the riots in July 1981. Also of note is the grandfather of the Duchess of Cambridge, Ronald Goldsmith, who had his wedding reception at this pub. The gasholder is to be demolished in the near future.

The Canal, Southall

The rather ramshackle buildings pictured on the right-hand bank of the canal were probably outbuildings belonging to Glebe Farm. The farmer was John Spark, who was married with two daughters and a son. He died in March 1923 and left the farm to his wife, Mary Ann Spark. Owing to its remoteness, Glebe Farm was one of the last in Southall, existing up until the early 1930s. The Grand Junction Arms public house is situated not far from the bridge; the current bridge dates to 1931.

Recreation Ground & Band Stand, Southall.

Recreation Ground and Band Stand, Southall

Originally known as Bill's Charity Land, the recreation ground became Southall's first park, opening in 1903. Mr Harman was the first park-keeper. In 1911 the grounds were extended by a further 7 acres. The bandstand and lodge were situated at the north-western section of the grounds near to Florence Road. The park is close to the Grand Union Canal and, during drainage excavations, a spur off the main canal was unearthed, possibly showing that the canal serviced the local brickfields, and the remains of a buried canal barge were found. The spur also serviced the original Southall gasworks that stood to the east of Florence Road, north of the park. The current photograph shows that the lodge remains but the bandstand has now gone.

CANAL SIDE, SOUTHALL.

Canal Side, Southall

Victoria Dock near North Hyde was built for the Sanders Tube Works. The entrance to the dock can be seen here on the towing path pictured around 1900. The Sanders Tube Works moved from Notting Hill to Gordon Road in Southall in 1901. Adelaide Dock is further along the towing path, near to the cottage painted in white that can be seen above the wall in the distance. Note the dense vegetation on the other side of the canal and the boy fishing. The current photo shows the spot where Victoria Dock used to be, having been filled in long ago.

Canal Side & Norwood Bridge   Southall

Canal Side and Norwood Bridge

The former Robinsons flour mill at Norwood was destroyed by fire on the 31 January 1912, despite the proximity of so much water. This image shows the mill in 1909. Norwood Bridge can be seen not far from the mill in the centre of the picture. The original bridge dates from around 1800 but a new bridge constructed in ferroconcrete was opened on 25 July 1925. It was built under the supervision of the local engineer and surveyor Mr J. B. Thompson. The current photo shows the building that replaced the mill reflects the prior building.

W. V. Taylor, Norwood Road, Southall

William Vincent Taylor is listed in the 1914 census as a 'shopkeeper', also owning a newsagents at No. 1 Manor Cottages, The Green, Southall. The shop seen in this image was at No. 2 Norwood Road and was taken over in 1920 by a Mr Thomas Pairman, a stationer. Apart from this shop, Mr Taylor also owned another newsagents, at No. 1 King Street, in Southall, which still existed in the 1930s. Norwood Road has since been renumbered and what was No. 2 is now No. 10, a timber and builders merchants owned by the Kallha Brothers, with a wider frontage than Mr Taylor's shop.

Clifton Road Schools, Southall

Sir Ralph Littler CB, KC, opened Clifton Road School on the 14 January 1904. This was a two-storey building costing £9,500; each floor had a central hall and seven classrooms, accommodating 800 pupils. Miss Becks was the headmistress of the infants and Miss Wilson was her counterpart of the juniors. Mr Elias was head of the boys. The staff and pupils of Norwood Bridge School were transferred to Clifton Road in 1904 and the former school closed. Note in the current photograph that the wooden fencing on the right-hand side of the picture has now been replaced.

Norwood Bridge, Norwood Green

Norwood Bridge was opened on 25 July 1925. This image is from the 1960s. The bus going over the bridge is probably the No. 232 that went from Greenford to Hounslow via Southall. In the modern photograph, a No. 120 bus going towards Yeading can be seen. This is the only bus that now crosses the bridge. The former Norwood mills once stood near this bridge but unfortunately burnt down in a devastating fire in January 1912. The Lamb public house stands close to the bridge, although out of view in the picture.

Norwood Green Grocers

This original photograph shows the grocery store and proprietor, believed to be Mr William Henry Hugh Wenn, at No. 151 Norwood Green. Mr Wenn was born in 1882 and was in the grocery trade for fifty years. He died on 27 November 1953 in Hillingdon County Hospital at the age of seventy-one, and his funeral took place at Mortlake Crematorium. Note the neatly stacked and well-organised shop window and the reflection showing the opposite side of the road in the plate glass. Norman's supermarket has now replaced this former shop.

The Wolf Inn, Norwood Green

Even though the public house sign for the Wolf Inn can be seen, the pub itself is out of view to the extreme right. Norwood Road was once named Wolf Lane, which may explain the naming of this hostelry. Although labelled Norwood Green, strictly speaking this scene shows Frogmore Green, the little green that appears on both sides of the road. The shop on the left was owned by Samuel Fenemore, a grocer and provisions merchant. The view must predate 1911 as he moved to Egham in that year and died in 1935. The current photograph shows that a hair and beauty salon and Ace Cutz now occupy the former site.

Police Station, Norwood Green, Southall.

The Police Station, Norwood Green

The Manor Farmhouse once stood on this site, owned by Thomas Walton and demolished around 1886. The present police station opened on the 16 June 1890. In 1894 the superintendent was Charles Hunt and there were also a sergeant and fourteen constables. The Norwood Green Police Station was a sectional station in 'T' Division. During the 1960s the police station was closed at night, but the public could use a telephone located in the front garden to contact the main police station in Southall. The station finally closed in 2008 and the police now operate from two houses in Norwood Road near to Wimborne Road. The building has now been converted into flats.

Dutch Canal on Norwood Green

The Dutch canal, lined with elm trees, can be seen in this view of Norwood Green from around 1900. Viewed through the trees where the ladies are holding their bicycles is 'Sunnyside', a Grade II-listed eighteenth-century house. The house is a rare survivor and Isambard Kingdom Brunel is reputed to have stayed here while working on his GWR project. The house has now been divided into two properties: 'The Friars' and 'Lawn House'. In 1928 the Dutch canal was filled in when the road was widened, but the main reason for this was that rubbish dumped into it had rendered it insanitary. The elm trees succumbed to disease and were felled in 1977.

NORWOOD RECTORY, SOUTHALL.

Norwood Rectory

The old rectory at Norwood dated to the eighteenth century and was described as being large and opulent. Elisha Biscoe, who founded the Norwood Free School, contributed to the building of the rectory. It had seventeen rooms, with a large drawing room and dining room, a study, lounge, two kitchens, pantry, bathroom and several bedrooms. In 1821, 5 acres were attached to the property. It was destroyed by a V1 rocket on 18 June 1944, sadly killing Gladys Saunders, the rector's daughter. The modern photograph shows the less-grand replacement rectory.

Norwood Green, Southall.

Norwood Hall, Norwood Green

On the left of this picture from 1905 is a significant, but possibly little-known, building comissioned by Sir John Soane, later known as Norwood Hall. It was built in 1801–03 for Soane's business associate John Robins, an auctioneer and estate agent. The house was irrevocably disfigured in the Victorian period when it was pebble-dashed and an extension was added. In 1956 it became the Institute of Horticultural Education, providing lectures on gardening. In 2001 the building became the Khalsa Primary School, a voluntary-aided Sikh school catering for three to eleven year olds.

Norwood Church

St Mary the Virgin Church in Tentelow Lane was founded in the Middle Ages. However, as Norwood still came under Hayes, it was not until 1859 that a separate ecclesiastical parish was formed in Norwood and connections with Hayes were severed. This former chapel of ease to Hayes was rebuilt in 1439 and again in 1864. Notable monuments include those to the Cheesmans and Merricks. The image shown here is from 1904 and has an interesting message on the back of the card, saying that the sender of the card attended a harvest thanksgiving service at this church given by the Revd Joseph Frederic Vincent Lee of Cranford 'who preached a most sweet and interesting sermon'. The current photo shows that the foliage above the wall has gone and a table tomb revealed.

PLOUGH INN, NORWOOD GREEN, SOUTHALL.

Plough Inn, Norwood Green

It is often stated that the Plough Inn dates back to 1348 but there is no evidence for this; the inn first appears in the local directories in 1845. It was substantially renovated in 1926, but the structure of the older building is still evident in today's building. This colourful image from 1907 probably depicts a delivery of ales from the brewery arriving on the left-hand side. The current photograph shows that the entrance porch has now gone, and the building has been extended on the right. The baskets of flowers give an attractive and inviting charm to this establishment.

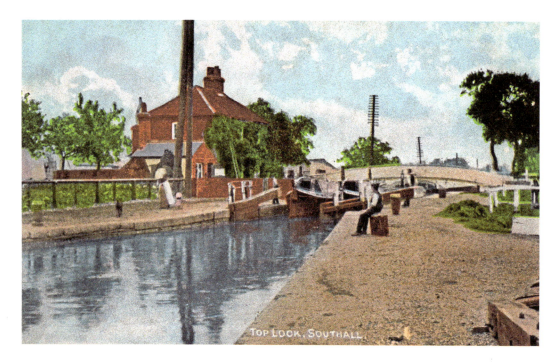

Top Lock, Southall

The 'Top Lock' is Lock 92 and is the highest lock on this particular stretch of the canal. The locks after it travel downwards to 97 in order so that the canal can reach the same level as the Brent into which it flows. In this Edwardian view, Glade Lane Bridge (Lock 204) is on the right-hand side. Note the large wooden mooring bollards that have since been replaced. The lock-keeper's cottage is an attractive feature. The British Waterways yard no longer exists and has now been redeveloped for housing while retaining the original house as part of the development.